ABOUT THE AUTHOR

Evrah Rose is a Wrexham born and raised poet and spoken word performer. A self-aware and passionate activist, Evrah uses her own experience and the experiences of others to tell rhythmic and hard-hitting truths about child sexual abuse, addiction, gender inequality and mental health. Evrah began writing at age 9 as a form of therapy to combat the hardship she was suffering. Some 20 years on Evrah has truly honed her craft, becoming one of Wales most prolific spoken word performers. Her work has been featured on most BBC platforms including BBC Two, BBC Three and BBC Four racking up nearly 5 million views on social media alongside television and radio coverage by BBC Wales News and BBC Radio Wales. Evrah is a regular contributor for BBC Sesh, writing and creating spoken word films. Evrah has performed all over the North West headlining shows such as Wrexfest, Apples and Snakes DiVerse #7 and Born Lippy as well as performing to thousands of fans at a Wrexham AFC match. Evrah has strong links with her local community, she is a trustee for the Venture, a playground she spent much time at as a child, she runs a multitude of workshops in and around her locality. She is a poet for Outside In at Glyndwr University and Poet in Residence at Wrexham AFC. Evrah aims is to use her poetry to raise awareness, evoke conversation and elicit social change.

Website: https://evrahrosepoetry.co.uk/
Twitter: @EvrahRose
Facebook: EvrahRose
Instagram: evrahrosepoetry/

Evrah Rose
Unspoken

VERVE
POETRY PRESS
BIRMINGHAM

PUBLISHED BY VERVE POETRY PRESS
https://vervepoetrypress.com
mail@vervepoetrypress.com

All rights reserved
© 2019 Evrah Rose

The right of Evrah Rose to be identified as author of this work has been asserted in accordance with section 77 of the Copyright, Designs and Patents Act 1988.

No part of this work may be reproduced, stored or transmitted in any form or by any means, graphic, electronic, recorded or mechanical, without the prior written permission of the publisher.

FIRST PUBLISHED SEP 2019

Printed and bound in the UK
by Imprint Digital, Exeter

ISBN: 978-1-912565-25-2

*Love is a cure,
an incurable disease.*

CONTENTS

Queens Park	11
Amy	14
Fathers	18
Ice and Water	19
The Barman	21
Waste Land	24
Do I have Depression?	27
Manhood	29
Our Tomorrow	31
Luck	34
Postcodes	35
Walls	37
Our Education	38
Ring O' Roses	41
Ancestors	43
The City	44
Power	46
The Sky is Ours	47
Labels	49
I Ain't Got no Money	51
Eton Mess	55
Rubber Bands	56
Somewhere In-between	58

Coma	60
The Shadow Beneath the Door	61
Sisters	65
The Trouble With Having a Vigina	66
Planes in the Sky	67
War Crime	68
Brittle Bones	70
Slithering	73
Seven Days	75
Mania	77
Didn't Mean to Hurt Her	78
Their Land	82
If God Were a Woman	83
Pin Stripe	85
Asylum	88
Skin Deep	93
F	94
Ballot Babies	95
Hyposhits	97
I Am Not Laughing	98
Who. We. Are	100
Blind Faith	105
Mind E-state	107

Evrah Introduces Ben Wilson

Acknowledgements

Unspoken

Queens Park

I come from nothing, 'they say'.
hailed from a world without silver spoon
diamonds or pearls
just humble beginnings
in a small council house.

Please, don't confuse what I am talking about
our community is worth more than gold
without a doubt.
Supporting one another - taking care of each other,
my friends' mother; was my mother,
and I loved that.

That's the thing,
nobody sees the way the strings attach,
they just want to blame and attack, branding us all with
the same dirty brush, without any prior fact.

Apparently,
we are all 'lazy criminals'
our grace is minimal
their opinions are cynical
without any knowledge, or fair representation.

Some of the hardest working people I know
have come from that estate
that coupled with strength and morality
is a hell of a combination.

We fight off stereotypes daily
they refer to us with condemnation
just to add to our frustrations
we are higher, than their estimations.

How many people can say they know their neighbours
on a first name basis?
Or walk into homes with open doors to be greeted
as one of the family?
Chit-chat at bus stops with friendly faces
always willing to engage - it's
these moments, that I am grateful for.

Gentlemen opening doors to shop floors
and best believe we will congregate in back yards to party
laughter and jokes nobody knows how to have fun
Like us. folk.

If there is a death - we rally around.
The impact is felt by all of us.
If Mrs. Roberts needs help with her shopping,
one of our youth will not think twice about stopping.
They aren't thugs, they aren't taking drugs
just merely being young.

The newsagent, knows everyone individually
and saves your magazine weekly.
Best believe she still sells ten penny sweeties.

Mike the milkman lends you a hand
lets you have milk on tick to pay when you can.
We have some of the most intellectual people hailing from our sands.
Our streets are littered with gratitude for the things that we have.
Not burnt out cars and stumped out fags!

We have pride in our homes
Mr. Davies and his large Gnomes.
hedge hopping, snow globes, youth clubs and snow days
a multitude of parks where children play
and some say...
Our communities are dumb plagued.

Well, let me tell you the truth.
We are proud people
we are strong and undivided
hard working, intelligent and undeterred.
Focused, driven, we don't forget our roots
course hands and worker boots.

Keep spreading your lies
your myths.
Coming from a council estate
doesn't make me poor
It makes
me
rich.

Amy

Amy rises from her chair late evening to look through the crooked slats in her blinds.
As cars pass slowly and the streetlights begin to illuminate. It's quarter past eight, it's nearly dark.
Her eldest child Kaylee woefully exclaims that she doesn't want her to work tonight. She's twelve years old and will be alone to fend for her two younger siblings, Hannah and Tyrone.
Amy looks back, that old familiar stare of sadness with a likeness to her father, those eyes and facial structures, the dent in the nose, her lip moves just like his when it quivers. It's enough to make Amy shiver.
She tells them their father is dead. Their father was an addict just like Amy, a violent one at that, beating her every day until she found her escape.
Six years on, she still finds herself stuck between a rock and a hard place. Her addiction has created a scarred face.
Amy was once so beautiful, she had the longest, blondest hair, ocean blue eyes and a complexion that could incite jealous hays whenever she glanced or gazed.
Now her hair is dry and old - she's grazed and cold - her eyes fold - cheeks are holed - teeth are mold - she's only twenty-seven years old...
She looks fifty.

Amy didn't have the best start in life, her father began to abuse her when she was just five, her mother, an alcoholic, abuse was rife.
Moving from home to home - squat to squat - eviction to eviction - lock to lock.

Each school brought with it the same old story, bullied from the
school gates to the classroom hallways.
She was the 'skanky child - pissy pants - shit stains - nitty Nance'.
All of which was fueled by parent's complaints to the teachers.
They shrugged and believed the lies, when her parents said she was
hard to raise as she was a difficult child.
Her body bruises were so easy to hide, underneath stained
and soiled clothing.
Not one of those adults became a beseecher, but, her grandmother
Rita.
She would bathe Amy and feed her with love so unconditional,
her liquid gold touch had no limit, but her father made sure, Rita
could barely visit.
Amy held on to those secrets, never to be told, while the one issue
staring at her,
Rita was getting old.

At thirteen, Rita passed, and Amy was passed from pillar to post.
That is when, during all the chaos, she met Jerome.
Whom showered her with gifts and a love she had never known,
promised her the world and gave her a home. He was, double
her age.

One evening, he introduced her to three men, Luke, John and Ben.
He claimed she should show the same 'love' to his friends, if she
didn't, he wouldn't pay her rent. She was vulnerable –
impressionable - she was condemned, with every week came more
of them, weeks were the same - end to end,
until she was pregnant at fifteen, to a man in his fifties, who
introduced her to that crack pen, in his crack den, to take away the
pain in her head, he said.
Years went by and two more children followed, until her body
was grey and hollow.

Kaylee sheds tears, she believes mum has worked at the club for years. Amy doesn't want to leave but has little choice with little voice, if she strays in any way, she will be confronted by the 'boys'

Amy isn't pouring drinks for money, she is selling her soul, her body, the only way she knows.
Most occupations, lack navigation towards those with zero-qualifications, plus, they just don't pay enough, and Amy, must pay Derek.
She best not cause any more altercations this week, she already owes him triple her salary, Derek is a "friend" of the family.
He's always around the house taking money, he calls it his "savings" bank.
'I'll take care of you all once I've built up enough cash', he says.

He turns up on a Saturday night and Monday morning, always with gifts for the kids. Amy cries, but they just never get it, they have so much love for their 'uncle' Derek.
He's a smart man in snappy suits and shiny shoes, hair gel and Gucci too.
Derek has a special infinity for Kaylee, she looks just like her mother, Amy.
Amy picks up her bag, moves her hair from her face and adjusts her bust and skirt.
'Be good now won't you, I'll be back when it's light'.
It's half past nine.

Amy works the corner of Oxford road with her good friend Bernice - they take care of each other - keeping eyes out for the police. If a client acts up, they bell Reece, that's how it works with those three in the streets. Protection doesn't always go to plan some days, Amy got herself a black eye last Sunday. He tried to take advantage and she said no, without any explanation you know how that goes.

At 12.23 am a punter pulls up, dark hair with his crisp shirt buttoned up.
He drives Amy down to the old dock and swiftly gets down
to business when she tries to leave, he tells her he isn't finished.
Locked. Doors.

He demands her money, before she can leave the car, he smacks her in the face and grabs her by the arm. The force of the struggles sets off the car alarm, this respected man doesn't want folk to become alarmed,
He takes her by the throat and squeezes until she screams no more. Dumping her to the floor.

He Revs up his Mercedes and drives away, leaving Amy's lifeless body in the rain,
dirt to face.
The children now alone, with no one to explain, while Derek continues to visit every day.
They have no way or room to complain,
'I give you all you need', he says,
'Be quiet or I'll send you away',
as he grooms Kaylee, and the cycle begins yet again.

Fathers

Father's treat your daughters well.
For her first impression of men,
will be her only impression.

Ice and Water

White shirt kind of man
crisp suit and tie
he could charm the legs off anyone
crimson smile.

He drinks whiskey from a crystal glass
ice and water
each key in his pin stripe pocket has Columbia
written upon it

he sees his dealer more than he sees his daughter
When she was 8
she fell from a jungle gym
he could have caught her
only his phone was more important
she is still scarred at the chin
a subtle reminder
that blood is thin

a businessman
never one to say no
to a gram
or a party
or prostitute
and the exes he holds hostage too

dick pics in abundance
none to his wife
who spends most of her time
waiting for him to arrive
dinner cold
another "late night" at the office

comes home smelling of cigarettes
cheap perfume and booze
calls her a slut as she leaves the room
he's horny and angry too
the type to assume
consent

self-entitled,
content
in his own filth
refers to women
as whore or bitch
The fifth of six
born
from a rich prick
whose morals
are
a quick trick
to buy whomever he
wishes
the watch on his wrist is
worth more
than time with his family.

The Barman

I watched you
half cut stumble into the doorway
legs bending at the knee,
the sun seared the red brick of your house
I could smell the tarmac melting beneath our feet
cementing itself
into my memory

you'd been at it all day
no work and all play
you splurged those benefits,
but you didn't benefit from any of it
the bar man did
truth hurts... in all ways

the hallway seemed never ending to your living room
that smelled of old cigarettes
you fell on to the sofa,
fag smoke made delicate pirouettes
circling the room that was a littered mess,
old cans and whiskey bottles
you'd preach lessons of life like you were Aristotle
I barely learnt a thing
only to never lay my foot at the throttle when half cut
I saw the way you drove
wheels all over the road
hands shaking,
driving the wrong way over roundabouts towards the groves
putting everyone in danger

and what's strange is I knew you well,
but you became a stranger
the more the years passed by,
becoming unrecognizable
undistinguishable from the strength I always knew
and the depth in which it grew,
stronger   and   stronger
I'd like to say your days grew longer but they got
shorter   and   shorter
a little less time with your son and daughters

your wife fell too but you couldn't have caught her
not in your state
there was nothing you could do for her
and nothing she could do for you
as much as you'd call her

did we fail you?
could we have tried harder to save you?
in death are you quenched?
or do you still gasp on the sand?
dry mouthed with flagon in hand?
do you still shake as you stand?
are there doorways you shoulder barge?

you were a two headed collision of cars
too much wreckage to salvage
you had time and you halved it
your last lines were tarnished

I watched you,
hard done I stumbled in your doorway
legs bending at the knee
the sun never appeared in autumn skies
over the bed that you were bound
I could smell disease leaking from your sheets
cementing itself into my memory

you'd been crying all day
all ache and all pain
you splurged those remnants of life
but you didn't benefit from any of it
the barman did

truth hurts, always

Waste Land

When Ben was a little boy, he wanted to be an astronaut.
he would fly homemade rockets around his living room,
there was no stopping his dreams.
NASA badges glued to t-shirts and jeans
that he had cut out of old magazines.

he would collect space rocks from the garden
hang planets from his walls.
and pretend that every hole in his door was a black hole of some sort.
that is how his imagination worked

scattered glass were tiny stars that would glitter in the light,
spilled coffee resembled galaxies at night.
And when the full moon shone bright,
he would glance out of his stained window in awe.

he had adult dreams at four.
a work ethic of a racehorse
and tiny hands that had become course.
he was a worker Bee.
something many had never seen, before
not at that age

school was a place of hate,
when he'd leave at the end of the day,
he'd go home to parents who still had rent to pay.
and not a penny existed between two hands,
just violence from fists that only exist to harm.

liquor bottles and syringes,
empty cupboards and thin ribs,
that could be played like an instrument,
his bruises were the markings of many incidents,
the insolence of parents who didn't really,
give a shit.
they had their own reality to deal with.

he would rummage in bin bags to fill his stomach,
scraping the bottoms of empty tin cans for something other,
than moldy bread.
neighbours would swear his parents would kill each other one day,
yet not one of them spoke up for Ben.

he was left to rot like the blood on his stained floors.
and he carried that
as he grew, he carried their silence into teenage delinquency.
car and store theft in unprecedented frequency
they wondered why Ben had lost all sense of common decency.

he was angry at his parent's decay,
society's lack of care he'd say
were his reasons for becoming everything other than his dreams
There is no opportunity in poverty
homeless, betrayed, he feels shame!

Police hate him
there's a call every week,
he would never confess,
 just merely regress into the mess that surrounds him

Until he found his calm,
in the back of an old car.
they said he'd feel warmth, and he did, in his heart.
his pain seemed to cease, his fingertips, stroked his scars.
a lightness in his face that had always been hard.
the most settled he had ever been with needle in arm.
his fists unclenched, his breathing, shallowed amongst
burning stars.

this is what it takes in our ignorant society
people must break in order to be heard,
people must die before lessons are learned
it's absurd
and now
he is no longer of a world defaced by disgrace,
away from this waste land,
Ben has finally become a space man.

Do I Have Depression?

It is like something gripping your throat
your lungs try to inhale but they can't cope with the weight
baring down on your
fractured chest
ribs puncturing you
pockets of air seep out until there is no breathe left
and while you struggle to breathe
you use your fragmented pieces of energy to long
for death

the world loses its colour until there is nothing but grey
you wanna' scream but you have nothing to say
because you feel that your words are worth nothing
your worth is of less
no self-esteem
no confidence
just
irrelevance

you feel guilty for being alive
shame when you can't disguise the pain within your eyes
you feel a burden to everyone around you
lagging behind
you look above and wonder if heaven really exists
because this - must be hell
and the fire burns your skin
your eyes swell yet you lack the motivation to cry
crying would mean you are alive when thoughts that suicide

would be the better
option
because let's face it
you will quickly be
forgotten
that's what your mind - has you believe

there is no relief
you don't sleep and when you do - you don't dream
your days lack meaning - your nights
are
endless
you are the shadow - lingering in family pictures
while they smile
you just
exist in this
cycle of pain
you lose your way striving to regain your health
but you are lost - afraid to ask for help
because they will judge - or never understand
yet this cruelty uses underhand tactics to force you to your
bruised knees
until you are trying to find your reflection in broken mirrors
and you stand there - staring - not knowing who you are
you bleed - hoping somewhere someone will hear your
silent pleas
in summer you freeze
your bones cold filled with tension
too terrified to ask yourself that unforgiving question
do I have, depression?

Manhood

Don't be so weak
when you speak
do it with authority.
Don't let them see the tears in your eyes,
son
you need to realise that to be a man
you need to keep that fear inside.

Or in time,
you'll lose respect from your peers
don't be soft lad
only girls cry
leave the emotions to the fairies.

This is what it means to be a man
you must show strength
and don't forget, he said
as his son dried his face,
unable to speak, a child yet already he,
was being manipulated by the toxic ideology
that manhood is about masculinity.

Time and time again,
our boys are forced to become men,
time and time again
we lose our brothers broken mother's cry for one another
these tear drops don't fill the silence
they must endure to look proud,
hold that certain demure that's damaging.

It's ravaging our society.
The profanity of crying.
Giving themselves
but doing it quietly.

Because our generations of stiff up a lip
have forced sickness into our kids
who believe that strength,
comes from a mouth clenched.

Our Tomorrow

Why do we patronize our youth - tell them to act like adults yet
treat them like children?
Old enough to consent to sex - yet lack the 'maturity' to have a say
on who to elect
where is the respect?
can't drink yet, they can gamble
scratch cards by the handful
are those lottery tickets the devils need to tease them?
another way to ensure their freedom is restricted of freedom?

they need people who won't deceive them
someone who will believe - in them
who won't leave them - neglected
make them feel respected
and protected
from stigma
and stereotypes that call them criminals for wearing certain clothes
hanging out on certain roads
saying certain words
acting in certain modes

mood swings and hormones
used as a weapon it threatens their validity when they speak out
like their decisions are indecision based on a rash heart
and over sensitive feelings
it's time we started receding our judgement
our prejudice is damaging to their self-esteem
when we disregard their voice
we warp their identity

Until eventually
that inactivity of self-belief becomes a self-fulfilled prophecy

our forgotten teens are the ones who will someday run
our country
pay our taxes
treat our families
path our roads
scatter our ashes
do you want confidence or outright backless?

because it's our actions towards our young
that will determine if prosperity is awarded to the few
or the masses
It's your decision
for our searching existential questions our youth have answers

Its madness
to know our teens, walk with such defeat in their strides
society beats the imagination - creativity and autonomy
out of their insides until they are nothing more than dead eyed
we treat them like property
tell them to stand up properly when they slouch
what if your back was aching from the sheer weight
of expectation?
let's see how you'd stand

we need to show love to our young people
show passion for their dreams
encourage them
lift them up off their knees

show them that we believe
in them
that they are not forgotten
give them a role model to follow
because in truth
this entire life is borrowed
and today's youth
are our tomorrow.

Luck

Their hearts - were few that day
as if the ground wasn't dry enough
Crisp yellow grass - under dying feet
young lovers - there to try their luck
in a land that many had perished
nothing to cherish - but small picture frames
with fractured glass
hands made to dig through dirt
that buries it's self - under fingernails
a reminder that - life is a temporary stay
for the moment - February can wait

winter is betrayal for tributary veins
wains for those who gave themselves
for pride - and for country
yet their flag - hangs in flames.
war brides are more hungry
for time
than food
mortality - is crude
a feud that began - with young hearts.
hoping to reclaim - themselves

and now
their hearts - are few today
as if the ground wasn't dry enough
crisp grass - under dying feet
young lovers
no longer try - their luck.

Postcodes

Welcome to 2019
where police restrain black teens - for no apparent basis.
This country is being intruded by hatred from racists
Neo-Nazi hooligans - look at the communities they are
breaking.

The government remains empty eyed and vacant to the blatant abuse
of our multicultural
nation.
That system deals the cards but holds all the aces
acres of land yet we don't have any spaces
for refugee families
I dare even one of you - trade places.

They've made this - country a fortress
barricade our borders
what if it were your sons or daughters?
Are you forgetting the lessons world war one and two taught us?
That division
will never reward us.

I hear chants of 'go back to where you came from'
was it the same song when we asked these communities to rebuild
our cities and towns?
somehow - our memory has faded now

it's a pity how
we eat their food and buy their clothes
watch their programs
and attend their shows (as long as it's benefiting us) right?

It's a hypocritical time and the media doesn't represent plight in
the way that it should be
Scare tactics
they're active in spreading maliciousness
dishing up viciousness to would be militants whose melanin is rich
in privilege
what's the difference
between one lung and another exactly?
Our skins cover the same anatomy
the only differing fact - is geography.

Location is everything
and if you're lucky enough to be born into postcodes that shimmer
consider the bigger picture
these 'strangers' are your brothers and sisters
and this
is family business.

Walls

If these walls could talk.
What if they could? She asks.
Would they recite children's screams?
adult voices whom spill blood from lasso mouths;
that grapple one another?

Would they speak of alcohol stained skin?
scattered cigarette butts
and blood-soaked floors?

Would they needlessly try
to mop up the coffee from mugs
thrown at such a velocity
they broke the sound barrier.

How about the locked doors that let nobody in?
and the ignorant neighbours who's voices
never spoke seedlings of truth.

These walls are paper thin.

She'd rather they stay silent.
She thought.
Just like them.

Our Education

Emily is a whizz at geography
Max excels at math's
yet the pair of them sit in class
wondering how they will pass their exams.

See, Emily doesn't understand equations,
Max can't read a map,
but that doesn't mean they aren't intellects,
please believe that they can
they have their strengths,
just like every child has.

We are preached to from an early age
about equality
to respect diversity
that not everyone is the same,
yet when it comes to exams
children are degraded by grades.

Expectation is too much to place
on a growing mind.
Why is creativity considered an academic crime?
The system lies to children and it's fine in their eyes.

You wonder why there's so many children in detention
Because they don't receive enough attention.
The youth are neglected,
misrepresented

not to mention the apprehension
they suffer from a system –
that seeks to define their worth
placing percentages and grades above their minds
like neon signs on conveyer belts.

If a child obtains an A in one subject and E's in another
does that automatically mean they have failed then?
No.
When a child bases their worth based on statistics,
it means we - have failed them.

How many times
has Pythagoras helped you fix your car?
Decipher your tax? Or pay your bills?
The school's curriculum is outdated and missing life skills
yet, they try still
to achieve that piece of paper
that tells them they are better
or worse
than their peers.

The exam system is plagued by fear
night sweats and tears,
yet they believe that is a suitable environment
for children to demonstrate their knowledge.

These tests are designed in one way
as if children have one brain
think at one stage

and their entire education boils down
to ninety minutes
and
twenty questions
for that one grade
one day

they will look back at their education with regret
for not only were they oppressed
they were taught in a way
that enabled them
to forget.

Ring O' Roses

Ring O' Ring O' roses, we all, fall, down
Children sing aloud as they fall to the ground
hands on chests
laughter rings
from benches to swings
every child lost
in imagination, it seems
as scents of spring, fill the air.

Proud parents standing at gates
as chit chat is shared
math grades and special awards
gold stickers and glitter cards
glue stains and grazes in school yards.
These are precious moments
(for the most part)
as they wave goodbye
another mundane Monday
as the hours go by.

Ring O, Ring O, roses we all fall down.
children sing aloud,
as they fall to the ground,
hands to heads
gun shots ring
from benches to swings
every child lost
in vain, it seems

as scents of gun powder
fill the air

Bereaved parents standing at gates
as tears and pain are shared
mass graves
special awards
no more stickers
and glitter cards
blood stains and hatred
on school yards
These are the moments they are left with
ghost hearts
as they wave goodbye
another bloody Monday
in America's cities and towns
Two shots.
Three shots.
Four shots.
Five!
Ring O, Ring O, roses
They all
fell
down.

Ancestors

You want to talk about diversity
like your ancestors didn't engrave themselves
into the palms of those of other skins
broke their shins
their backs
and gave them names
that erased their ancestry

you want to scream patriotism
like this land was always yours
you cannot own - what you stole

you wear brands as if machine made cotton
always handed you clothes
like floors where never home
they traded faces for gold
races were sold in - chains

traces of your past still live on
when you brand their youth with delinquency
within the frequency of deaths and arrests
prisons filled with minorities
in a whitewashed system
isn't 400 years long enough?
It seems that crime is only crime if the melanin
is strong enough.

The City

The city never sleeps
its eyes stay bloodshot wide like a cocaine high,
shaking to feel again
step on them' streets you wouldn't believe
the types of dreams that rise from knees
begging to breathe.

There is no release
its inhabitants are imprisoned to its promise of success
it seems
their thoughts are rich in the same expectation that traps them in
to 9-5s
beggar's belief
Renters in need
the working man is poor queueing at food banks at the weekend –
the breadline
poverty is hereditary amongst everyone
but the elite
ingraining itself into - unsuspecting families
this is our society undeniably it's lying to each
one of us

graffiti lines the walls - women walk to cat calls
down streets of scaffold towers
man songs whistled from way up signal intent
yet
nothing screams fear like a woman
walking alone while being verbally savaged
misogyny in crass forms

a place where men indulge in mass brawls on Saturday nights
at kick out time
masculinity can only be demonstrated by a flexed arm and
bruised eye
because pride - is worth more than pride

minorities run from authorities; policies lack in honesty
and honestly - its racism
these are the people in charge of 'great' Great Britain
agendas in motion - remain hidden
rights remain displaced race remains victim
they want to beat our people into submission
they create fear out of religion
separating us from each other
just listen to our talk of division

they tell us - be vigilant
be wary of the villainous
any time now an attack could be imminent
deliberate in prejudice
step back people here comes an immigrant
scrap humanity
treat them like a criminal
the city
has become cynical.

Power

For every insecure woman stands a man
with flowers.
For every insecure man
stands a woman
with power.

The Sky is Ours

We can only be divided if we allow ourselves to be confined to our own ideals. Our own predispositions degrade our societies. Equality, is unafforded unless we share the wealth of freedom that some, more than others have the luxury to taste. We are parted by gender, our segregation leads to hate, I can't bear to face the state of this world. Our ignorance makes us blind, closed eyes to the suffering of who we define as strangers, of varying ages and faces. But we need changes

Women told they are ugly in dresses our expectations cause stresses to young minds, configured to undermine their self-esteem. Crop tops and skinny jeans sexualized as teens. Photo shop destroying our belief in ourselves. The ridiculous standards that we call beauty. A term exchanged for confidence that doesn't exist in our realms. Speaking up is unattractive, ensuring we don't break our chains, we are enslaved, to this unattainable imagery, pushed upon us before we can even walk

I've seen men choke on their own pain, sacrificing themselves for what we call manhood. No man should have to face depression alone, crying is considered weak, when to breathe is a feat too obscure to achieve, we'd rather our men bleed than be anything other than this masculinity forced fed since birth. When will we learn? When will we stop killing our brothers with silence, the violent white noise that clenches their lips, too terrified to reveal the struggle within, we scrutinise. We can't lose any more men to suicide.

Why do we have to conform? Why do we have to perform to this deformed and warped ideology. Pink for girls and blue for boys, man up, gender specific toys, it's a ploy deployed to sanction us, branding us so we don't think outside of the box they have for us. Why do we have to lay ourselves on chopping blocks for being different. Gender is just a figment of our imagination. Why do we have to die in order to seek autonomy, why are we still trapped within inequality? Why are men barely surviving trying to be strong? Why are women striving for these fucked up ideals? Period poverty, FGM, we have both genders hiding for fear of shame defining them.

I long for an uprising, sisters and brothers of many skin colours do not stand divided. Do not fear the hour, look above and see the sky for what it really is
Ours.

Labels

The circularity of elitism
a sweet prison of
self-satisfaction and unsatisfactory behavior
that we, as the poor, pay for.
We spend our souls so they can make more

where is Robin Hood?
robbing hoods
flogging goods on street corners
made by the very people that inflict his impoverished torture.

He passes these labels on to his teenage daughter
whom fought her sisters for clean water in the bath
four in the same tub,
plus
Mum and Dad.

Water should not be a luxury in this country
we have one of the richest economies,
yet we have working families living in poverty,
in poorly heated properties
that landlords rent out extortionately
and if you can't pay your rent, you can pay with sex,
we have people living disproportionately
and you expect crime to descend
in a society where the wealthiest get everything for free?

Loopholes ensure they increase their equity
while Jo from down the street
works excessively
to pay their taxes,
enabling MP's to claim expenses,
and they wonder why society detests these
politicians?
Because they are relentless in their agendas to serve themselves
don't ask us why we cause you hell
and protest as well –

we are so sick of you
Here's a different view;

The next time you see our people selling goods in the street
from five fingered discounts, hoodies and jeans
just remember whose name is on the label,
blood in the seams,
woven from the cotton of greed
manipulating trade with the rottenest of dreams,
sold to the people forgotten by tweeds.
They aren't scum
they have needs.

I ain't got no money

I ain't got no money.
I said
I ain't got no money.
They ask me of what currency do I speak,
I speak broke, honey.

Shredded pockets and knee ripped jeans,
I can't afford this tee',
I wear it like a medal of honour, something I worked to achieve,
materialism... will be the death of me

is this a joke? You want me to part with this 20?
How am I gonna' eat?
Maybe I should lose a few pounds
just like the magazines
and become raggedy but skinny Anne,
as thin as I already am,
I can't be thin enough
my gap isn't big enough
I don't quite make the cut.

They label me anorexic in return,
because I
don't have the beauty to make heads turn,
take a picture of me
you can guarantee
that shit will get burned
unless it's vetted by me
first.

Filtered - structured - saturated - the big three
but still as good as those filters make me think I look

I have no fucking money

I don't have that 50 for those jeans
I wear Primarni G's
these baggy things cost me 11.90
they wash poorly - fit me badly
but that's all I can afford
these
days...

I live by the thin of my waste cause'
I can't live enough on the livable minimum wage
doing the horses work while somebody else gets paid
I am the modern rideable slave
working their residual - individual trades
so they can see the dividends in their pay
while work/work/work away.

I have a strong back
But when I leave at the end of the day
I ache
Physically – mentally – emotionally
I am drained
but that's ok

because they got one hundreds' to buy those shoes
while mine are cheap, hole ridden and abused
from treading painful steps for their ruse.

The harder I grind - the bigger the tax
the more I strive - the more they take back
educate yourself - and they personally attack
the pockets of the minds - who want their freedom intact.

Keeping us in that tax bracket
that crap-basket
where we know little of the opportunity that lies before us
I ain't asking,
it's mad if
we snub the debt riddled education system
they will continue to adore us
enough to make us believe that what they do
is done for us
when in truth
there is no reward for us.

It's all a trap
to keep you locked into that benefits cap.
Cap it enough to afford you the bread line,
give you enough to keep you to a deadline
the dead-line at the job centre
where you are fed lies
from the dead eyes
of those corporation
head guys,
I see it as a trend guy's

not one of them is there to represent I
to represent you
so be mindful of your youth
they will come to take that too

national service - is seemingly unheard of
but I know the truth
we are still slaving and trading our lives
for their gold loot
their war boots
they got us good
they hold me
and best believe
they own you too.

Eton Mess

Skilled workers - lay in traps,
caught in snares, trolls live under bridges tax-ing the poor man
until he is forced to live off the state
dependency.

Not out of will - but neccesity.
Feed yourself or your family, you cannot do both,

You may be skilled but you can not do hope
Hope is what they take at job centre,
To ensure you don't revolt.

Devote your life to your work and you will pay with your home,
They will take from you as you age.
And at this rate, health care will belong to the rich
God help us if we ever get sick
Brick by brick they will build a wall to exclude us
But there is more of us than there is of them
And what they don't realise is we are on the rise
That idea is beginning to materialise
There is fear in their eyes
It shows in their manner, in their quarrelling
They can't make a decision without borrowing
The deficit is theirs not ours
And we've saved up more than enough man hours to elicit their defeat
Because regardless of what they try to make us believe
They CAN NOT STOP OUR BEA

Rubber bands

They say they want to clean up our streets
to encourage better feet
those who speak with differing accents
the kind that pronounce, their 'T's'.
What's wrong with a glass of wa'er?
We still tease those syllables.

I don't see them sitting down with
any street men and women trying to understand.
They just spend rubber bands and leave.
Point marking benches,
so that he or she
must move on
and become someone else's 'problem'.

They say they can't 'solve them'.
There is far too little income generation
to help.
Not enough circular.
Instead
they lay new pavements in our Centre
Insert soothing light fixtures into the concrete
remove chewing gum from the roads
add geranium to our roundabouts.

The aim is
to rejuvenate
apparently.

Black paint and barbed wire
rails between seats
pay fines for not being,
discreet.
New bricks for the elite
Not enough sterling
to enable them to eat.

Somewhere In-between

I remember just looking into his stained eyes and seeing nothing but pain, the light had gone. The years had finally caught him in the cruelest of ways. His battle had been long.
See, time is a currency we are handed when we are born. Some of us, are given bags full, while others, live hand to mouth. He was always somewhere in-between.

Yet, he overspent. If only I could have given him a loan! But the world doesn't work like that.
Time again we begged him to stop, but he just couldn't. His life had been awash with unsurmountable pain caused by the very hands of his father, whose abuse was always followed with a beating after. He became a martyr through necessity, brought up in a society, with a sweep it under the carpet mentality, eventually, his own mind became his enemy, that held him hostage. Until he found his escape

Drop by drop he swallowed the darkness oozing from his pores, the dirtiness the thoughts he so badly wanted to rid him self of... and he'd pour another and other until he was numb.
And that's how he spent his adult years. Avoiding reality. Slumped over the sink cigarette in hand, sweats and shaking needing just one more sip.
Until his last kiss, dry lipped.
He was given five days and fought for seven.
I watched strength drain from him minute by minute. Slowly poisoned by his own body, his skin turned a shade of murky yellow.

I played him music, we held his hand, kissed him on the forehead and told him to sleep, that the family would be alright, and it was ok for him to leave. He left, almost in peace.
Empty bottles lay in the recycling with his fingerprints still smeared upon the glass. I wanted to grasp them so tightly, because at least in some way, I could still hold, his hand.

Now, we look through damaged photographs, we didn't take enough pictures, the ones we have are old and disfigured. Here's to wishing, he was with us. So, we could capture one more memory, Christmas and Birthday's.
I'll never be able to stop the feelings of guilt and shame; I'm reminded each day that he could have been saved. And for those reasons, I can't visit his grave.

Because, even though we tried, are we the ones to blame?
We hated his love, but he loved the pain.

Coma

Have you ever watched a man die?
To take his aching last breathes right before
your bland eyes
Have you ever seen a grown man crawl on his knees and cry?
Wail in excruciating pain with his hands high
begging not to be shot
one more time

do you know what it's like to see strength evaporate before youth?
and youth to dismantle before you?
tell me the truth
have you witnessed the screams of children carrying a corpse
through sands of broken glass?
that buries itself into their tiny feet - their tiny hearts
to carry that weight too far that it breaks
their backs
have you?
seen blood spill from lips and limbs
kicks to shins
bins full of paper memories burnt for fuel

because the past kills for fun
he had nowhere to run
the devil caught him too young.
Children mourn what they never had
as he lies in a body bag
have you ever watched a man die?
well I have.

The Shadow Beneath the Door

Mummy, can you hear me?
Mummy, can you hear me?

I'm sorry I was bad tonight
I'm sorry I'm bad every night
I don't mean to be
but I don't understand how to speak
of the monster that frightens me

footsteps
there are always
footsteps

I wait for that sound and they always come
casting shadows within the light beneath my door
can you hear the hinges creak as the door slowly swings open?
and the delicate treads on the floorboards until they meet my bed?
I lay there still,
bereft

my covers are pressed firmly against my face
just shy of smothering myself
my legs coiled around them
like a boa I constrict
if I stay stiff enough and my movements are minimal
maybe this time
I will become
Invisible

the monster always finds me
stronger than I
the covers are little more than a sheet of paper
being ripped from me and thrown to the side to reveal the rubbish beneath
I am
a worthless piece of meat

I don't have the strength to fight anymore and it's better to stay quiet
I can't even remember what a tear is
I haven't cried in a long while
you always talk of how good I am
Oh, she never makes a sound - she never causes a riot
but I have no sounds
words completely evade me
I'm too young to understand
I just know that I don't like it
it hurts
Mummy
save me.

I tried to tell you yesterday as the monster watched
eyes piercing through me
ravaging my ability to communicate rationally
I stumbled over the inaudible sentence until each syllable was but air
I exhaled
and once again my mouth was held closed
laid bare
'Mummy won't love you if you tell her'
Do you love me mummy?
Will you love me?

I've stopped talking
I don't want to be alone so it's better if I don't
nobody notices anyway - too busy with their own lives
their own groans
Mummy do you see me?
Do you see the dark circles around my ageing eyes?
I shouldn't be so old - I'm only a child

Teachers are dubious but they don't want to assume
why a child seems to have such fear of the moon
why I'm withdrawn
missing too many days of school
or why I don't play like the other children do.

I momentarily forget as I play in the park
when the streetlights come on
I'm filled with the stark
reminder that it will be bedtime soon
and so, comes the monster with the rising of the moon

I know I'm a good girl for the most part
I always finish my dinner Mum; I always do what you ask
I never hurt my sisters or call them nasty names
I do my schoolwork
the bed
the dishes
I try my best - every day
I'm sorry if I make bedtimes so difficult
I'm sorry I sap you of your energy
I am not a bad child
I am not the anti-Christ
I am not your enemy

I'm just trying in the only way I know how to make you
hear and see
the crippling pain that has been burdening me
if you look closely, I am transparent
just like glass
open your eyes - see the cracks
don't let another sunset pass
and if you never do anything
then all that I ask,
Mummy, please
don't put me in the dark
don't put me
in the dark.

Sisters

For every
silent
tongue
sits a girl
somewhere in this world
wondering
why her sisters
betray her.

The Trouble with Having a Vagina

There is no liberty, our wombs percolate for profit,
dare we speckle your sheets for this
will incite disgrace
and disgust of our deposits,
yet, aren't we your mother's?
Did we not raise your brothers who love us for our purified silk?
You shame our nature,
humiliate us
like you've never tasted our milk and our honey does not feed
your acres.

Planes in the sky

She made angels - out of those tracks in the sky
what else could she do
with those innocent eyes?
Try to distinguish reality from dream?
As a child,
it is much easier to live. a lie.

Imagination comes in bundles,
in vines
at times
colours come alive

red is a pigment - washed upon their skins.
As they lie,
on bricks,
splinters to shins,
to limbs
time stills,
as that familiar hum lacerates the air
fire in their rain
those angels
come in pairs

and there, she stands,
a lone flower,
unassuming; armed with one last petal.
That will fall to the earth
to the sound
of machine gun metal.

War Crime

We scroll through endless feeds
thumbs stroking cheap glass
we can't get enough of these - bleak ads
that encourage us to feel bad

Insecurity is worth more than confidence quietly
we flick between windows
 it's almost monotonous

videos of dogs in Darth Vader suits
cats wearing shoes
the condom challenge
 images of poorly prepared soup
(because everyone is a chef and a photographer these days)

we are distracted from reality
truth
armor and muddy boots
in fields of fallen youths
violence and torture
isn't good enough for our news
when will it be good enough?
when our humanity is hanging by a noose? when the white West is finally affected by it too?

I can't stand the hypocritical waves from this
raw tide
that somehow
we

are entitled to more time
governments and media fill us with poor lies and statue
lips cost more lives
because silence isn't just ignorance
my people
It's a war crime.

Brittle Bones

Why do you not want me?
Do I not taste the same?
Do my thighs not invite you -
the way they did those first days -
when your thirst was too much to take?

Did you drink enough of me somehow?
is my hair too long now?
(Because we both know, you like it short).

Am I no longer in your thoughts?
The type that stir you in the night
and force you to linger in corridors with fingertips
that long
to choke
every single last breath from lungs
that are too weak to grasp
at the air

the girl with the fair
skin
and blue eyes
a prize that you have sought
all this time
yet now

I am obsolete
I am no longer surplus to your needs.
You have fed from me,

sucked the innocence from my brittle bones
that have splintered
and cracked,
and crumbled - for your enjoyment.

You have taken the fire from my retinas
and replaced it
with charcoal,
these sockets have become black holes
that kill even the bravest sparks of light
that dare to enter

You are the poisonous water
that bathes me
ten shades of dirty

You told me,
to never tell
You taught me
silence...
The hand over mouth,
dare I move,
breathe loudly,
just close my eyes
and
pray
that it's quick
this time
type of silence.

How loud it can be
How deaf the world seemed
when I learned to scream
quietly

and finally
as streams of red emerged
a surge of adolescence
purged your thirst
that was once nursed by bare flesh
and a slender waist
mature became
a bitter taste.

Slithering

I live an augmented reality
With my imperfect intervals,
like they were inserted into my internals
I'm an absentee
finding no satisfaction in this mundane existence
just like this world before and after me,

I lay my ashes and pieces upon this mantelpiece,
I'm needing something to anchor me,
that doesn't aim to dismantle me,
My face is mapped in a way that compartmentalizes everything,
like an amputee
I'm limbless

I feel the pain stretch through my core into my fingers,
and it lingers, like a foul smell,
I don't spend these hours well,
Seconds are wasted, time has no time for time,
step in to this world of mine,
give me a sentence and I'll share half a line
as long as twine denouncing this frame of mine,
that has become crooked and old in age,

I stand on stage as a joker faking love by masking rage,
my masquerade is a half a shade darker than my soul,
I take the longest route alone,
for my home, is not a home.

It's more of a dome of imprisonment,
where my thoughts collect and assemble
and obscure my envisionment,
I am needing something to envisage,
someone to listen to reduce the diminishment
of my omnipotence,
I'm living this,
day by day I'm carried away into the distance
away from my former self that I'm hidden within,

living a sin without giving a whim,
I feel the net closing within an inch,
I'm giving in
I'm giving in.

So, don't crawl inside of my withered skin,
where winters been and snakes are slithering,
whispering and differing in their indifference
for the world they have me living in,
I'll just continue play the fool,
without admitting it.

Seven Days

I saw you, hiding behind his mother,
as she gently made her way to the car,
over a mountain of white flowers and cards.
frozen January skies had cried for the 7th day,
to this present day, I still remember the rain.
cascading in the most somber of ways, as if even
the earth felt pain.
and she moved,
with a tremendous weight,
as if her body was too heavy to hold.

I'd seen that same look before, in him.
her stare was very much akin.
It was as if I was staring into the same eyes,
the only difference was the faint lines of time.
and she seemed to have acquired a few more.
she was ageing before us as if a second was a century,
and she wore it in his memory.
while you stood, watching her tirelessly.
sapping life from her bones.

the street was in mourning.
heads low.
parents didn't know how to explain you to their children.
so, they didn't.
they hid away from the truth.
because you made age out of youth.
she had barely moved from her living room.

curtains remained closed with only fragments of light
seeping through
the gaps in the window.
her lights were always on.
maybe it was to help him find his way back home,
while streetlamps stood as maps to her door.
but nothing shone brighter than that fluorescent blue.
creating shadows that jumped from one heart to the next.
his father hit the ground and screamed
a sound so pain stricken it would never leave my memory.
clouds of life evaporated from his soul.

no one felt the cold.
I ran in to the street in my pajamas.
I didn't need to be told. I just knew.
even at twelve I had strong intuition.
and I saw you in that street.
fleeing the scene, guilt free.
those flashing lights slowly disappeared,
and neighbours made their way back to their families unified.
while you
began to reside with his mother parasitically unsupervised.
It was the first time I heard your name,
you buried yourself into my ears and skin
like a diseased tick
you stayed with me into that night
you are with me to this very day.
You have no care over human life
depression calls and you are only too happy to oblige
I have seen too many of my peers
over my short years
succumb to you
suicide.

Mania

It is like balancing a tight rope
from one helium balloon to the other
without reigns or safety nets
knowing that at any moment you could fall to your death
yet
spinning anyway
without the melancholy of regret.

Didn't Mean to Hurt Her

I know you didn't mean to hurt her.
Her skirt was way above her knees and when she bent over,
you could see
all the way into heaven
her ass clapped to the beat
every time she moved her feet,
her breasts bounced loose
like they were dancing for you
and her nipples
they stood erect through that low
buttoned
white
shirt.

I know, you didn't mean to hurt her.

As she laughed and played with her hair
every time
you'd stare
glanced every five minutes
to check that you were still there,
as she twisted and jived with her friends,
her seduction
had no end.

She was fine
and juicy
as they come

her skin looked supple
as if layered with silk
and rippled like a firm jelly.

You could feel the fire burn in your loins
you longed for a moment with her
a tenderness to nurture

I know you didn't mean to hurt her.

When you,
made an overly aggressive pass
and she refused
so, you pilled' up her liquor
to lower
her inhibitions
to your seduction
under the general admission
if she says no
you will be an embarrassment to your mates
your assumptions of which
stood in abundance

I know, you didn't mean to hurt her

When you thrusted her lifeless body animalistically
until she could stand no more
until
she fell to the floor
head sinking like an anvil
crashing down

she said
STOP
but you never heard her.

I know, you didn't mean to hurt her

When you
pulled her hair
and
called her slut
because
she didn't suck good enough
she was off her face in many ways
she didn't want that kind of love
nor did she want to be touched
it was tough
you decided
she deserved it rough
this girl is getting 'stuffed'
thank you very much.

You left her alone in an alley
for some stranger to unearth her
at night.
You didn't mean to hurt her,
right?
Cause'
how dare she flaunt what she has
to tease you,
Flaunt what she has,
but never bought you,

all of which,
to 'taunt you'
those legs,
those thighs,
those hips,
those eyes
How dare she not know
that she
did not have the privilege
to say
NO
you didn't mean to hurt her
did you though?

Their Land

Run! Just. Run!
Were the screams she charged to
bare footed in blood stained dress
plumes descended from barrel
one after another - grazing her ears
pelting her sisters and brothers
as sun seared their skins
a deeper shade of colour
screams echoed - from rocks - to sky
her movements were slow motion
as her feet swept up the dry
dust clouds at her heels
their anger amplified
with scopes of accuracy
for they won't be defied
two shots.
three shots.
four shots.
FIVE.

If God Were a Woman

If God were a woman
would she be praised in the same way?
depicted in the same state
or have her rights stolen - every single day?
If God were a woman - would she have gone to school?
Would she have been afforded the same opportunities as men?
Or would she be forced to her knees - time again - whipped
and chained - from toe to head?
Would everyone hang on every word she had ever said
like gospel?
Would she have been honoured for her breasts
and reproductive abilities?
Rather than forced to give up - her bodily - autonomy?

Would her womb be sacred?
Would her choices be respected?
Would she be loved as she is naked - without makeup
or computerized imaging
to enhance her already beautiful frame?

If God were a woman - would you ask her
where's my dinner?
Would she be filling plates?
As a child would she have played freely?
Sun on back - eyes to the horizon - would you see thee -
in a different light?

If God were a woman
would she have to fight to have her voice heard?
Would she be banished from her society simply for being female?
Would you love her for every detail that makes her unique?
Would she be allowed to age gracefully?
Would the lines on her face be worshipped for wisdom?
Would she have to work 8 until 8 shifts for half the pay?
Aching her back trying to raise three children alone
barely paying rent for her home - making ends-meat to survive
the rain
would she have to offer her body in exchange for currency to fund
her way through university?

If God were a woman - would she be raped?
Have her testimony denied and her perpetrator escape
because he is an honorable man to his community
while she bleeds from the gut
cut - by agonizing cut
If God were a woman
If God were a woman
If God were a woman

She would still be a slut

Pin Stripe

She stares at the poorly painted white walls that surround her
completely numb.
As a woman in pin stripe scribbles on a notepad.

She clutches her coat,
bag and shirt
her throat twangs painfully every syllable
her feet clench, between each breath
a clock ticks', it's 3.am.

She watches
as every word is carefully written on to
creased paper
she has become a statistic.
Ten minutes was all it took
to change her
from a happy light-footed woman,
to a stranger that her family barely recognize.

She was an A grade university student
with goals and ambition
tenacity and vision
yet, one mindless act
has made her body a prison.

She wonders how she will ever get clean
falls to her grazed knees
and cries.
Head in hands as she lies on the cold floor

this was the day she died
wounds soar
that room saw
a promising twenty-year-old become
an empty corpse.
A shell of nothingness.
Nothing could heal her pain
and slowly as the days went by
she could no longer sustain the lie that she was fine.

She stopped leaving the house
stopped answering her phone
wanting the world
to leave her alone.

they did,
they stopped calling, stopped knocking
she craved so badly to feel something
other than shame
she found that solace
in a blade.

Her skin became a maze or scars
a razor can't erase the past
yet, she tries.

Her bed is her home now,
she hasn't eaten in weeks.
Her hair -
unwashed -
slimmer waist -
stained sheets.

Every time she closes her eyes, she relives the scenes
she can hear her own screams
flash backs invade her dreams
and sleep
has become a memory.
She finds no relief
succumbing to PTSD.

Yet, they blame her
and shame her
for the clothing she wore -
label her a whore
(and more)

portrayed as a liar
they wonder why so many retire
from the courts system.
CPS drops the case
another walks free - to violate again
justice is missing
an ocean of contradiction
I guess they see Laura
as just another victim.

Asylum

Look at me. Please. Look at me
for I am in crisis
glance away from your phone
the Wi-Fi, the wireless,
the Insta, the Facebook
see that I am in high stress.

These feet have circled a thousand steps
in my night dress
this noise is too much to digest
I'm tense
somebody break-down my fence
where I scream
from my mess
the jumbled-up thoughts that kill
my sense
the shadows
the voices
the night sweats
in a room where I've wept
a thousand times

before a mirror covered in paper.
Too fearful to look myself in the eye,
for I see the evil lurking inside
Maiming my body,
I know that in time
this body will no longer be mine

Doctors, nurses
I see you are underpaid and unappreciated
your funding depleted,
but please
hear us cry
for we are defeated,
you
are needed,

but you just
stand there and stare
without whim or care,
the 6 c's no longer there
Package of care neglected for tales of new hair
drunken weekends
you are unprepared

While screams are heard from corridors,
as we bleed from the horror of doors
without handles
sinks without taps
meshed windows and showers without caps
bland rooms with poorly painted walls
and badly cleaned floors
not even hand wash to bathe our hands after the toilet

yet you act like you spoil us with a frequently locked pool table,
it's there to toy with us,
with hints of normality
it's there to reward us should we act sane and shut up
because, as you say, you have 'work' to do.

You say you're busy but I'm yet to see you move
from your nurses' station
it leaves me bemused how observation can be done in separate rooms
we are left to bruise while you are completely amused
by your own company.

No sympathy or empathy just rusty weeds in an unpruned garden
where we sit and smoke for hours with our evident distress,
because you have other interests
you have other staff members to impress
with your Facebook posts

you groan when you answer the phone
to be greeted with moans of disgruntled family members
because this is unlike the therapeutic home
that you stipulate
more of a prison facility.

They are infused with your apparent fragility
your lack of humility
where is the morality?
I know you have long hours and families to feed
broken backs and wage decrease
but that doesn't mean you can ignore us
when we bleed
and use medication rounds to obtain peace
Fill us with medication until
we sleep
and you can finally watch TV without a whimper or creep
these lips were made to speak.

you make us believe that we are an irritant to your day
'Stop being a dick' came from the lips of a HCA
as he sat topless with muddled head
though he was crass and course
he was inhibited in thought
he was vulnerable
this ward has run a discourse
when foul language is used as a fragrance

you lack patience with patients
you argue with them instead
lay hands upon them with intent
and deny the touch like you are innocent

I may be what you define as obscure
yet, I can see straight through your core
and there's nothing there.

This is the NHS laid bare, roots of despair
mental health is underfunded the funding isn't shared
and I stand here in defiance
I thought asylums had been banished
your training has vanished,
and you fail to manage the smallest of tasks

we are all branded as crazy and if we speak up
our words are simply symptomology
something our hallucinations 'think up'.

You come out worse than when you arrive
leaving other services to pick up the pieces of that hell ride
that you - call therapeutic care.

What you are doing isn't right
complaints pushed aside
pain defined as annoyance and you hide behind your uniforms,
to you this is just employment
to us,
this is life
look inside
open your eyes to the plight
this is our fight, and you're making it difficult
don't shut us out with your laughter and poor excuses
when we request support and guidance – we matter,
just like you do
we have feelings
enough of the chatter
do something to help us declutter the clatter

I know you are unappreciated and underpaid
but when you leave work at the end of the day,
you leave a footprint that will outlast the words you do,
and don't say
the actions you prove,
that don't pay

because while you eat your tea,
we are stuck in this dome
wishing just like you
we could go home.

Skin Deep

Her confusion
spoke the woes of a thousand sisters
silent tongued
chained by the shallow expectations
of femininity
from womb - to grave
for knowledge
is as vulgar as hair
she glanced upon me with ashamed gratitude
as tears gently filled her eyes
it was the first time she was called beautiful
not for her skin
but for her mind.

F

Exams are the most insidious form of social control.
For as long as we can alphabetically and numerically
convince children they are stupid,
We reduce their power to change a system
That seeks to exploit and manipulate
their sense of worthlessness.

Ballot Babies

When people talk scrutiny about estates I usually sigh
but today is different the news is brutally right
and I can't help the fact it moved me to cry
three of the poorest wards in Wales on streets that used to be mine
poverty continues to rise the figures don't usually lie
grades decrease as our school money declines
as a result our young uns' opportunity's die
so don't patronise me and say my community's fine

It used to be my - treading ground
so my reaction needs to be said aloud
read in towns and neighboring cities, Chester bound
something for your ears to be bent around

I can't pretend the sound of MPs gassing over expenses doesn't make me irate
when our youth are being shortchanged at such a high rate
a deficit that the young pay for on my estate
and they deliberate over why some choose not to fly straight

crime rates can decline if adequate opportunities are afforded
yet, they put a price on education so most can't afford it
elitist curriculums, free school meals aborted
and you wonder why teens have so much anger towards it

restoring faith is so hard to do
when there are no activities for after school
cuts to the youth clubs that look after you

and suddenly you're living off half the food
ask the youths
they'll part with truth
serve you just desserts that are hard to chew,
hard for you to hear? Is that why you are stuttering
when you talk about governance and restructuring
when our teens ask you where all the funding is
you're dismissive and ageist, let me tell you something
wisdom doesn't come with age it comes with suffering
and we have 89 year old teenagers needing comforting
because their communities show no sign of recovering.
and while you enjoy lavishness, people are struggling.

Stomaching the reality that care is dissolved
unless of course there's a vote involved
it's called selective politics

just look at what they say they are abolishing
yet, never accomplish or acknowledge it
poverty, inequality in what they are (aren't) promising
their empty words are just astonishing
no action, no movement to abolish it
spewing garbage to our kids, while the world is stood watching it
It's all lies regardless of how you polish it
they see no point in acting if it's profitless.

Hyposhits

I hear them
erupting into racist laughter
over an Indian meal
while drinking French lager
their seats are made of fabric
woven in Ghana
and they drive off in German cars just after.

I Am Not Laughing

They stand there
laughing
from the pits of their stomachs
over a pint and some pork scratching's
as one of them grabs his nuts and continues
to jive
high fives all around and they sip
grinning

I caught beginning - middle and end
and I am not laughing
because women remember
what it's like to feel nails in back
thighs ripped apart
trousers torn
top stained
the growl at the nape of the neck
the heavy hands
and scent of aftershave that turns a Boots store into a flash-back
they must have forgotten to glance back

to catch the eye of not just one
but many survivors in the room
they must have forgotten
the wombs from which they were born
their mother's who were pinned against walls
their sisters who were upskirted in nightclub's
their partners who were groped in lift's

their friends
who are too afraid to walk alone at night
in carparks
at cinemas
down streets that are so familiar

that feel uncomfortable in meetings
at shops
checking their back seats in the car before they drive off
they must have forgot

but why would they remember
when they have no idea what it's like
to be a woman walking with keys in knuckles
wolf whistled
trapped in a prison of objectification
without the means to confidently say no - without repercussion

it was at this moment
I realized something
that nothing - would change
for as long as these toxic attitudes exist
I choke
Because

For women
rape is a reality
For them
It was just a fucking joke.

Who. We. Are

When I was a child, I had a dream to be a professional footballer.
One day when I asked to join a team, I was told no.
Disgruntled fathers would not accept their sons playing with a little girl, football was,
for boys

why don't you play with dolls? I was asked,
why don't you wear a dress?
why don't you act like a girl should act?
I didn't react,
I started trying to do my hair - wear makeup
and behave like the other girls in my class.
But it just wasn't me.

It's funny how I was so young,
yet my body was owned by other's opinions and today,
I see the same fate in others.
As women we are told we must be beautiful,
not successful
and if we are to be successful
we must do it beautifully.
If we possess leadership skills we are told we are bossy,
labelled a bitch.

We are told to mold ourselves
based on magazines
topless models on page three's
we have women hiding in toilets
to breast feed

because breasts - can only be hung free
when pleasure - is priority
although to feed is the most natural act that we can perform

we are told to cover up to conform
to the strict identity of modesty
yet males
can walk around topless and honestly,
it's degrading
to find yourself shaving every part of your skin
just to fit in
because hair is vulgar... apparently
even though it grows from birth
hair is as old as earth
we have more than worth
yet we are told in womb
we are degradable dirt.

We suffer from expectation
we are supposed to marry
we are supposed bare children
and if we don't,
we are barren.

There's not one country in this world that respects females
the same way they do males
regardless of our strengths and our qualities.
Make my dinner dear
be thinner there - be bigger here
grow your hair - paint your nails - change your face
consider here - this liposuction
or facial reconstruction
I'm sick of the assumptions that we are the weaker sex

damsel in distress
with little interest in anything other than
shoes
and that little black dress.

Did you know that only a third of our politicians are female?
How can democracy be demonstrated
with this significant detail?
Expressing the views of women
yet
they derail policies on domestic violence
forcing victims into silence
anti-abortion policies
and awfully they try to deny the occurrence of FGM
that prohibits women from experiencing pleasure
because dare a woman
be in touch with
her
sexuality

child marriage – rape - sexual abuse
this society is a noose from which
they wish us to hang.
Girls hiding in locker rooms
because they fear the shape of their own body's
and slang calls us
slut - whore - slag

Feminism
the idea of the political
social
and economic
equality

of
the
sexes
so stand with me in shirts – ties - skirts or dresses.
Whatever you are comfortable wearing,
release your scars and stretch marks
and remember
who you are

You are
Cleopatra,
a woman high in intellect and stature
changing the course of history
you matter.
Billie Jean fighting the stereotypical shuns of femininity
we have ingenuity and strength.

Alice parker heating homes and Kwolec with Kevlar,
saving lives every day.
We pathed the way for women in science
to scoop the first Nobel prize, Marie Curie.
Rosa Parks refused to give up her seat
for equality.

Dr Shirley Ann Jackson, caller ID.
Don't mind me, cause ain't I a woman?
Truths journey.
Grace Hopper - the first computer,
and surely that's enough to have you believe?
Sarah Mather, telescopes for submarines

stem cell research, Ann Tsukamoto,
sitting in the front row of the fight against cancer.

The discovery of DNA
Rosalind Franklin;
Amelia Earhart - the first female to fly solo across the Atlantic,
our history is gigantic.

Benazir Bhutto the first female to take charge
of a Muslim state.
Maryam Mirzakhani and the first Fields Medal,
Marie Stopes - sex ed and birth control.
Audrey Hepburn,
Oprah Winfrey,
Julie Walters,
Sibyl Sassoon,
Maya Angelo
we shall not be moved.

We may be discriminated
beaten and hated
segregated
we are powerful
innovative –
an inspiration

most of all
we
are
amazing.

Blind Faith

When you think about it, choice isn't logical
it's based on chance the moments of, sod it all
toss a coin mentality, it's comical
how many choices seem applaudable -
when in truth they are implausible

culpability is the lessons we teach our seeds
when our choices are made out selfishly
without considering the consequences carefully
and our minds only operate selectively

respectively some choices are made with rationality
yet others are made despite the harsh realities
it's mostly absent mindedness, actually

fractionally correct but often mistakes
that's choice, and it's ours to make
mostly made with blind faith
you should see how much mine fakes

why take too much time to reflect?
reject the idea of self-respect
until there is nothing left to represent
and he smoked his choice, a cigarette,
without the tip
and although he made the choice to end that relationship
by the time he'd kicked that habit, his body was a failing ship

saying this he says gasping for air is a lot like drowning
surrounded by air but you can't inhale what's around you
if you knew of his life it would astound you
instead all you see is a frail man, sofa bound too

I'm not allowed to cry over this in front of him
don't want to scare him or leave him wondering
if the end is sooner than the thunder is
because the lightning flashes right under him

numbering his days by the minute
forgetting he's still alive and with it
he may be slow, but he isn't finished
regardless of how much he's diminished

I wonder if he regrets the choices, he made
if he knew of mine, what would he say?
imperfection is in the finest detail
there are cracks in all of us equally, male and female

he saved a lot of his love for my gran
I have a lot of admiration because life can -
bring you challenges and failure, there's a high chance
if they can last 60 years in marriage, then I can

despite the rough they made is possible
and I'd say their choices were responsible
for them having each other so far down life's chronicle
together they have been unstoppable
there have been times where they could have lost it all
overcoming any and every obstacle
yet, choice is about as certain as improbability – it's almost illogical
at least we have the choice to believe in the improbable

Mind E-state

I grew up in social housing,
and I carry with me the fondest of memories.
A sense of being that I haven't quite been able to restore
since privately renting.
I don't know my neighbour
and quite often I make jokes about his peculiar behaviour
his visits to his shed in the early hours.
I couldn't ask him for a favour.

Not like I did in the past,
When neighbours in houses and flats
Came together
Open doors and welcome mats
Take me back
Where I was most content

Many see social housing as just a concept,
a resolution,
a project
yet, it is something more.
It is, providing families with
security,
stability
and the ability to thrive.
It is safety for our most vulnerable people.
Society has forgotten the route of social housing,
where we were once proud to say
we housed
heroes.

Where the health of our nation mattered
and those who could do something, did.

So as a Council estate kid,
I ask of you this,
to consider what a council estate is.

It is a place of activity,
of community
where people actively support one another.
Where generation after generation grow
and develop.
Where youth and age share stories,
of activism, hard work and glory.
A place my grandparents will live out
their last days.

It is not a crime scene,
an area of vulgarity that the media would have you to believe.
It is, a hand that helps you up,
a loving embrace,
a gentle kiss on the cheek,
a push to finish that race,
laughter,
a friendly voice at the end of the phone.

A place that enriches lives and warms
even the coldest bones.
Call it what you wish,
but remember this,
to you, it might just be an estate,
to me and millions more,
its home.

Evrah Introduces ...

Ben Wilson is without doubt one of the most talented wordsmiths I have ever heard. He is a kind, thoughtful and welcoming soul whose wordplay can only be described as mesmerising. Thank you for showing me nothing but support and encouragement along my journey. I am lucky to not only share stages with you, I also get to call you a friend.

Hands
by Ben Wilson

careers advice said
her hands were meant to be
typists, secretarial
hands to help men

she'd say:
'no, they were never'

they are a polite middle-finger-to-the-man
pint holding hands
page devouring, erudite travelers
riding fifteen-hands
wild-taming
caring, creative
never-complaining
and strong as a fucking tractor

wrist-war champions
which will still
drink every no-you-can't
under the table

and
his hands were meant to be

pit-head drills
gafferred to inked pistons
coal blackened, slag heap
tenement two-up, two-down
bread-and-dripping hands
back alley scrapping with
smashed milk bottles for fun

but his first action man was Armstrong
and he strummed Bowie on invisible strings

see
his hands have fairytales waiting at the end of every fingertip
wire-thin with magical creatures living in them

his hands are safe hands
they are playgrounds
they are slapstick-battling monsters with silly accents

his hands are so much more
than the story they are telling
they are the best storytellers ever

these are the hands that made me

               and if there is any good in mine
                           it can be found in the palm of theirs

SIDENOTE:

When people ask me why I don't write love poetry, I often laugh it off as the so called, Queen of Darkness. Yet the truth resides much deeper. It lies between the fear and vulnerability I experience when putting pen to paper (or fingertips to phone). My priority when writing anything is to break down some sort of barrier. To elicit change and conversation that could ultimately resculpture a set of ideas that have long been unchanged. To create an environment that respects everyone and validates all experience. And why do I do this? Because I love you. Yes you, and everyone else reading this. I care about society and what my fellow human beings suffer. I am passionate about the world, the issues that we as a species face. I am fortunate to have a skill that can bring people together and I am privileged enough to be have people listen. I must use that voice to the benefit of those who cannot speak, who have little rights and little choice. And for those who fought for my right to shout, to live. Without them, and you, this book would not exist. So in truth, I am a love poet, I write for love every single day.

ACKNOWLEDGEMENTS

Katie, I dedicate this to you. For the hours you have spent listening to the same poetry over and over, the endless road trips and the pick me ups when I've needed a boost of confidence. For your utter belief in my ability and your support in pursuing my dream. My best friend, incredible wife and overall favourite human. Thank you.

Adam, who pushed me to achieve when I needed a kick up the arse. You kickstarted what has been an incredible journey.

Stuart at Verve for having faith in my writing, being a trusted ear, advocate, friend and giving me the freedom to create.

And to you, the reader, the listener, the individual. Thank you, you are my biggest inspiration.

ABOUT VERVE POETRY PRESS

Verve Poetry Festival is a new press focussing intently on meeting a local need in Birmingham - a need for the vibrant poetry scene here in Brum to find a way to present itself to the poetry world via publication. Co-founded by Stuart Bartholomew and Amerah Saleh, it is publishing poets from all corners of the city - poets that represent the city's varied and energetic qualities and will communicate its many poetic stories.

Added to this is a colourful pamphlet series featuring poets who have previously performed at our sister festival - a poetry show series which captures the magic of longer poetry performance pieces by poets such as Polarbear, Matt Abbott and Second City Poets. But most importantly we are open to publishing anything that we feel demands to be in print, anyone whose words we feel need to be heard. Evrah Rose is just such a voice - earnest, lively and important.

Like the festival, we will strive to think about poetry in inclusive ways and embrace the multiplicity of approaches towards this glorious art.

www.vervepoetrypress.com
@VervePoetryPres
mail@vervepoetrypress.com